REAL ESTATE
AS A SECOND LANGUAGE

REAL ESTATE AS A SECOND LANGUAGE

A ridiculously authoritative dictionary of words and terms for anyone who owns, sells, buys, rents, builds, or has driven by real estate.

by Roger Reitzel

illustrated by David J. Schutten

editor-in-chief Lisa J. Reitzel

Chicago Review Press • 213 West Institute Place • Chicago Illinois

Library of Congress Cataloging in Publication Data

Reitzel, Roger.
Real estate as a second language.

"A ridiculously authoritative dictionary of words
and terms for anyone who owns, sells, buys, rents, builds,
or has driven by real estate."
1. Real estate business--Anecdotes, facetiae, satire,
etc. I. Schutten, David J. II. Title.
HD1379.R445 1983 333.33'0207 82-23507
ISBN 0-914091-21-2

First Edition
First Printing
Second Printing 1989

Published by Chicago Review Press
213 West Institute Place
Chicago, Illinois 60610

Typography by Siemens Communication Graphics

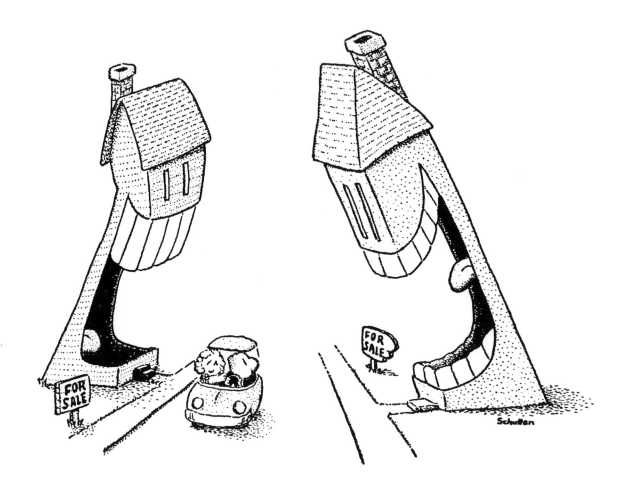

A

abandonment
A simple procedure used to divest oneself of real estate, it involves packing, leaving, and never coming back.

abstract
1) A full historical summary of all that affects title to a given parcel of real estate. 2) The manner in which an agent will answer specific questions. about the given parcel of real estate. For example, "Well, home values have certainly risen in the theoretical sense . . ."

acceleration clause
Clause used in a mortgage, installment note, or contract for deed that gives the lender the right to demand full payment upon the occurrence of a specific acceleration event, such as the mortgaged home doing 0 to 50 in 4.5 seconds. If the home in question is a houseboat, this is also known as a "due on sail" clause.

acre
A measure of land equal to 4,840 square yards. An acre may contain this yardage in any shape whatsoever, although acres that measure 10,560 by 4.13 feet are looked upon as unsuitable for all but the oddest of purposes. Considered a high-status lawn size, the acre is recognized as the primary reason for the invention of the riding mower.

agent
A courageous individual who insists on believing that he can support himself and his family by trying to sell that which nobody can afford to buy. The word is thought to be a derivation of a Greek word meaning "one who peddles what he does not own."

An agent actually works as an arm of the broker, although under certain circumstances he may also be allowed to act as a thigh. While an agent earns only a percentage of the total brokerage fee, the potential income in real estate sales actually is very high. However, unless the agent participates in transactions, this potential will not be realized. For this reason, you can go into any real estate office and find agents hard at work screaming at the phone, weeping softly to

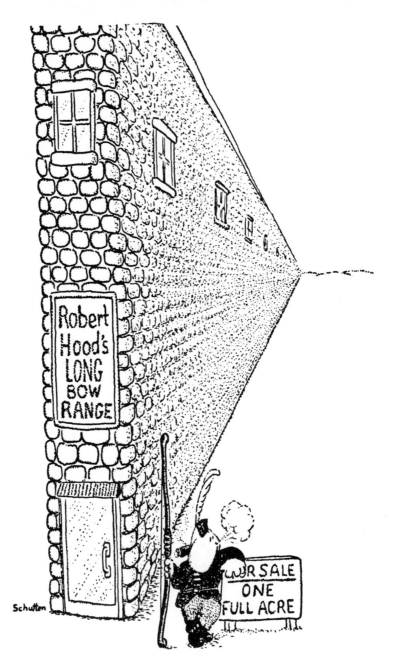

The odd acre has its uses.

themselves, doing crossword puzzles, sticking pins in little attorney dolls, and intensely debating the merits of possible establishments for midday nourishment.

AML
A form of home financing that allows the interest rate paid by the borrower to fluctuate according to specified indicators which could result in home-owners paying many years and owing more than was borrowed. What the letters stand for depends on whom you ask. The public contends the initials stand for Assured Money Loss, while the savings and loan industry prefers Amazingly Machi-avellian Lifesaver.

amortization
A rather amusing game concocted by mortgage lenders that is played by the following rules: First, they give you a whole bunch of money so you can buy a house and have someplace to live. Then, you send them some money every month so you can pay back what they gave you. Ok, here's the fun part. After you make these payments for three or four years, you find out that you've only reduced the amount you originally owed them a teensy tiny bit.

Now, if you keep playing, you'll find that by the time the amount is reduced by any noticeable degree, you'll be too old to make the pay-ments. And if you play the game to the very end, you'll wind up paying back many times what the house itself is worth. Say, isn't that a great game? Why do we have to play by the lenders' rules? Because it's their bat, their ball, and until that loan is paid off, it's their house, too.

anchor bolt
A type of fastener that, upon mal-function, will let your house float away.

apocalypse
The day your mortgage will be paid off.

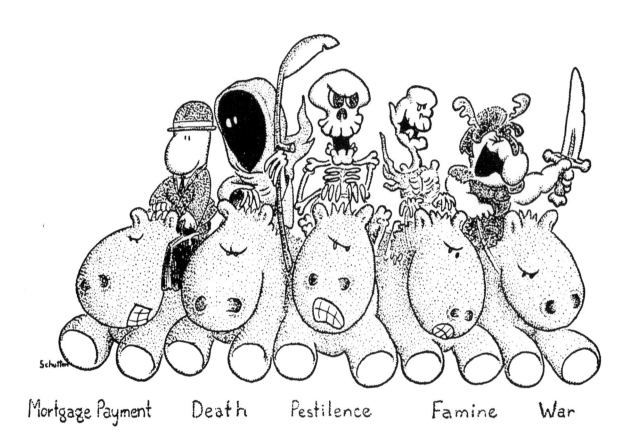

Mortgage Payment Death Pestilence Famine War

The five horsemen of the Apocalypse

appraisal

An estimate of property value based on factual information. These facts, however, are often merely estimates or opinions from other appraisers, the end result being the blind leading the very nearsighted.

An appraisal may be done using the market data approach, the cost approach, or the income approach. Any one of these methods will, with the appropriate manipulation, satisfactorily rationalize a good first hunch.

appraiser

One who compliments your house for money. Example: "Appraiser here, ma'am. Gee, this is a very lovely home! And what nice taste you have! That'll be sixty bucks, ma'am."

appreciation

An archaic term referring to real estate value direction.

articles of agreement

Used in certain areas of the country, a rider attached to a contract for deed. The less the buyer and seller agree on, the longer this rider will be.

asking price

It is well established that there are two things that Americans will just not pay asking price for: used homes and used cars. The only people who do pay asking price for a pre-owned home are those who are so incredibly wealthy that they can use that fact for status ("Oh, hell, we just decided to pay them what they wanted. After all, Poopsie just loved the breezeway and why quibble over a few hundred thou?") or those who are so incredibly stupid that they don't comprehend the tacit meaning of the term ("Well, see, if that's what they're asking, I guess that's what we'd better pay 'em, huh?")

assumption

Something one thinks one can do, such as take over another's backbreaking payments. This is known as a "false assumption."

attic

The open area in your home between the roof and the ceiling where you store that which is valuable, and where other family members keep that which should be thrown out.

attorney
An expensive lawyer (see lawyer).

B

balloon payment
1) The monetary consideration given to a vendor of inflatable rubber bags. 2) A method of financing real estate that allows buyers to float along lazily for three to five years and then suddenly bursts, sending them earthward where they will crash headfirst into reality, suffering both physical and fiscal ruin.

basement
Similar to attic, but capable of sustaining mushroom growth.

bathroom
This most private of all home areas is often referred to in terms of fractions such as "full bath" or "half bath." To clarify these fractions, a "full bath" includes a toilet, a sink, and a tub and/ or shower. A "half bath" has a toilet and a sink. Moreover, a "quarter bath" merely has a toilet, an "eighth bath" a sink, a "sixteenth bath" just a single faucet, and a "one thirty-second bath" contains but a lone toilet seat and is not recommended for large families.

bats
A type of ceiling insulation found in many attics, bats are considered inferior for the following reasons: first, they won't stay in one place long enough to do any good, and second, they rank among the noisiest of insulators, what with all that squeaking and flying around banging into stuff.

bay window
Pained glass that howls at the moon.

bearing wall
Wall that supports the floor, roof, or ceiling above it. If you are unsure about which walls in your home are actually bearing walls, try this simple test: raze the suspect wall. If you are killed in the process, it was probably a bearing wall.

Inadequate bathrooms meet buyer resistance.

Bedroom community

bedroom community
A town or neighborhood which is treated by its inhabitants as if it were one big bedroom. This includes not only individual homes, but all areas of business and recreation as well.

In a bedroom community, everyone is constantly in a rising or retiring mode, unshaven, groggy, and Oil of Olayed. It is quite customary to go to a restaurant wearing pj's and slippers, or to play racquetball in a fuzzy robe. Appealing as this may sound, there are two major drawbacks to such a community. First, everyone you come in contact with will have incredibly bad breath. Second, due to the fact that all areas of a neighborhood are used for "bedroom activities," the whole town may be deemed unsuitable for younger or more sensitive viewers.

bill of sale
A written instrument by which personal property is transferred from one owner to another. The bill of sale is the page in the sheaf of papers tossed about at a closing that indicates that all of the appliances and other items included in the transaction by the seller because they didn't quite function properly, are now the buyer's headache.

binder
That which those who have recently purchased real estate consume to relieve one of the various gastrointestinal disturbances that inevitably occur when they are faced with the reality of having to scrape together the impending monthly payments.

blanket coverage
A loan covering more than one item such as a home, a comforter, and a crazy quilt.

blended rate mortgage
A type of loan that takes the interest rate of the present mortgage on a home along with the prevailing market rate and arrives at a new figure by throwing them both into an Osterizer. The prospective buyer is usually more receptive to this blended rate if he is first offered a blended Scotch.

block busting

The illegal practice of inducing home-owners to sell their property at a low price by telling them the neighborhood is changing because someone nearby just sold a home to a family of blocks. Most people now realize, however, that having blocks in the community will have no negative effects. Being rather square, blocks are as a rule very quiet and generally just like to stay home and stack.

blueprint

An expensive, detailed architectural plan by which a home or other building is constructed.

Printed on heavy paper (quick, what color?), the blueprint must be handled with extreme care, for it is the working map for the onsite builders and is followed meticulously. The tiniest rip in the blueprint could result in a gaping hole in the family room, large enough to admit the elements, woodland creatures, or dreaded neighbors. By the same token, miraculous home repairs can be made using the blueprint and the local voodoo carpenter.

breezeway

A covered passage between the house and the garage where family members stop to chat.

bridge note

Temporary financing that helps home purchasers span the vast chasm between the time they buy a new home and the day they sell the old one. Of course, this is definitely a toll bridge.

broker

One who is licensed by the state to act as a representative for other parties in real estate transactions. This results in his having less money than some (the broke), but more money than others (the brokest).

BTU

An abbreviation for what the people of England must use in order to conserve precious heating fuel—British Thermal Underwear.

building permit

Written permission granted by the local public construction authorities that you didn't bother to get and would have never been issued anyway for that jerry-rigged disaster you call a "bonus room."

bungalow

A small 1- or 1½-story house, bigger than a cottage but not than a bread box.

buydown

A short-term financing plan that pays an upfront fee to the lender and thereby temporarily reduces the interest rate (and the payments) on a new, temporary loan. This is yet another method that allows the buyer to forestall for three to five years the inevitable "death by mortgage."

buyer

1) A person who actively solicits the help of real estate people, has no money nor the ability to raise same, and has not yet placed his present home on the market. 2) Any person who will give very specific guidelines to an agent about what a home must have to be considered for purchase, then proceeds to buy something entirely different from somebody else.

A reasonable person who has money, credit, sensible housing needs and wants, and has been transferred to a high-paying job starting immediately, will not be a buyer. Instead, this person will a) get hit by lightning on the doorstep of a real estate office; b) be hailed as the Second Coming and treated accordingly; or c) rent.

buyers' market

A term that, upon reaching the ears of most prospective home purchasers, induces them to go forth in search of housing by offering ridiculously low sums, using Gestapo bargaining tactics, and treating all sellers like members of a sub caste.

Cape Cod and occupants

C

calculator
An electronic device used to perform the precise mathematical functions that explain why you can't buy or sell a house in your present financial condition. Many of the computations used in today's real estate market could not be swiftly and accurately performed by the average agent. In those years B.C. (Before Calculator), an ancient real estate legend actually foretold of a tiny machine that the gods would send to take the place of brains.

Cape Ann
A small symmetrical 1½-story compact house with a central entrance.

Cape Cod
Similar to Cape Ann, but owned by fish.

capital improvement
The procedure by which one learns to make better big letters.

carport
A garage that makes it easier for someone to steal your power mulcher.

cash flow
The phenomenon of money rushing rapidly downstream in the wake of a real estate purchase.

caveat emptor
Latin, literally, "Let The Buyer Suck Eggs."

chattel
Derived from "cattle," now any personal property that eats grass.

chimney flashing
1) A strip of metal placed at the junction of the chimney and the roof to prevent water seepage. 2) A popular exhibitionist's hobby, common around Christmas.

clapboard
Appreciative house siding.

Chimney flashing

close to the train
Found within an ad for real estate, this phrase is intended to indicate easy access to public transportation. Upon closer examination, however, it instead explains why there is a crossing gate in the foyer.

closing
The culmination of a real estate transaction when the seller delivers title to the buyer in exchange for the purchase price, a closing is a fascinating event in which the fiercest of natural enemies are brought together in one small, improperly ventilated room. Come, let us journey together my friends, as we travel from start to finish through this dangerous yet enthralling ceremony.

At a date and time agreed upon by no one, the ranks file in. Within hours, the closing begins. The seller's attorney has hand delivered the batch of documents that were painstakingly prepared by his secretary for this very occasion. Slamming the sheaf downward, he blindfolds the seller in preparation for the signing of the papers. When this is completed, he swiftly gathers the papers and laterals the bundle to the buyer's attorney who is ripping the blindfold from the seller and placing it on the buyer for his turn at endorsement. When the last document is signed, the buyer is grabbed by the ankles and held upside down until the appropriate certified checks come forth. Throughout the entire procedure, the attending agents continue to repeat their submissive chant, "Can I get anyone more coffee?" Suddenly, the buyer, realizing he is the only one not on the receiving end of a check, becomes enraged. At this point, an official from the lending institution clubs the buyer to his knees with an amortization schedule and the closing is officially concluded.

closing statement
1) A declarative phrase used to finish a presentation, such as "And that's the way it was, July 7, 1980" or "Good night and God bless." 2) Any statement uttered by a participant at a real estate closing such as "But I haven't read those papers!" or "Hey, let go of my ankles!"

A true colonial house

cloud on title
A condition resulting from a visible collective of moisture particles enveloping the evidence of real estate ownership. This condition can often worsen and become the more serious "rain on title," rendering the title soggy and entirely unreadable.

cluster housing
Where grapes live.

colonial
A misused term that has come to describe almost any two-story house. But those among us who have any degree of architectural savvy know that for a home to be truly colonial, it must have shutters, a center entrance, be symmetrical in design, and contain one or more Pilgrims.

color of title
White, although some very old titles may appear yellowish due to age.

commingling
The illegal and perverse deviation of unrelated funds sharing common quarters, this act is performed not for money, but rather, by money.

commission
(a.k.a. broker's fee, brokerage commission, highway robbery) The compensation paid to a broker (customarily by the seller) for services rendered in connection with the sale or exchange of real estate. The amount is usually based on the sale price of the home and can range from 5 to 10 percent, depending on the type of property, local practice, and the gullibility of the seller. The exact rate, however, is subject to negotiation because fixed rates would be in violation of antitrust laws and we wouldn't want to do that now, would we?

Upon having to pay a commission, people have been known to express the sentiment that the agent makes more than does, for instance, a brain surgeon. But as any agent can testify, when dealing with an uncooperative and unreasonable client, it would be easier to replace his brain than change his mind.

Commingling: caught in the act

commuting

The process of having to spend more time and effort going to and from one's place of employment than one does while one is at one's place of employment. Commuting can be done by car (where one can glower at the anonymous idiots who are blocking his path) or by train (where one can sit directly beside those idiots, get to know them, and be annoyed at close range).

condominium

From the Latin word meaning "to share walls with those of lesser intelligence," it is a legal form of ownership of a unit located within a multiple unit development. In residential condominiums, this involves taking a large, comfortable living area, dividing it up until each resulting space is too small for habitation and then selling these tiny spaces for an unconscionable profit.

condo

Originally a shortened form of condominium, this word has had a strange evolution from a noun ("Hey baby, how's your condo?" or "There's no place like condo.") to an adverb ("My apartment just went condo." or "Her pants could definitely go condo!") and finally, to a verb ("Don't condo me, man!" or "I was born to condo.").

contemporary architecture

Any style of building that is ugly in a modern sort of way.

contingency

A provision in a contract that requires the completion of a stated event before that contract is binding. Very often an offer to purchase is dependent on obtaining financing. Example: "This contract is contingent upon the buyer's uncle passing away quietly in the night, leaving him untold riches." Occasionally, the buyer may make the contract contingent on the sale of his present home, which has come to be known as the "when hell freezes over" clause.

contract for deed

(a.k.a. land contract, installment contract) A form of creative financing in which the seller becomes the lender. While very attractive to the buyer, it can be extremely expensive for the seller who has to hire tellers, build a nice lobby, and install a drive-up window.

Cottage

conventional loan
See pipe dream.

coop
A shelter or enclosure for animals.

co-op
Structurally identical to above, but located in Manhattan and somewhat more expensive.

cooperating broker
One broker who helps another broker screw you into/out of a home.

cornice
1) The molded projection at the top of a wall, generally of a decorative nature. 2) A game hen with a lisp.

co-signer
When home purchase is imminent, this is a term of endearment directed toward solvent relatives.

cottage
A term used to describe any residence so small that even the most un-scrupulous agent would hesitate to call it a house.

crawl space
A form of basement for underprivileged midgets.

creative financing
Any of a number of methods used to purchase real estate that involve that which is illegal (in some areas the term includes armed robbery), immoral (for example, the contract sale with a three hour balloon), or merely weird (using shoes or kitchen appliances as down payment).

cul de sac
A street that goes nowhere, often found in subdivisions of the same fate.

curb appeal
Common in the present market, this is the art of a seller kneeling by the edge of the street in front of his already underpriced home and begging passersby for an offer of any kind.

Curb appeal

D

deed

A written instrument that conveys ownership in real estate, a deed is one of those forbidding legal documents that the home buying and selling public really doesn't understand. In actuality, deeds are quite simple. Why, you can even draw up your own deed. Here's how:

1) Buy some real expensive paper, the heavier the better. Attorneys have long known that impressive looking documents help create that aura of legitimacy and make it easier to justify the unreasonable cost.

2) Always use a typewriter. While handwritten deeds are valid, they tend to be messy and this negates the effect of the nice paper.

3) There must be a grantor and a grantee named in the deed. Grantor and grantee are the special legal spelling for Grandma and Grandpa. Mention their names somewhere in the paper and this should be sufficient, providing your spelling is correct.

4) A deed needs consideration. Place it gently in the typewriter, put the touch control on the lowest setting, and never fold it harshly.

5) There must be words of convey-ance in the deed, such as "here."

6) There must be a legal description of the property being conveyed. Here the law demands absolute accuracy, so be sure to include every number of the street address, as well as the color of the homes on either side of the property and the general condition of the landscaping.

7) A deed must be signed. Anyone handy can perform this task because nobody ever checks.

8) A deed must be delivered. If you can get a Boy Scout to perform this simple task, this will insure the document to be a "good deed."

9) The deed should be recorded, no matter how weak the melody.

That wasn't so hard, was it? Now if you just make sure that any deed you draw up in the future follows these few rules, you can not only save money on your own transactions, but help your friends, too, and be on your way to making big money in real estate.

Legal deed (cut along dotted line)

depreciation
A loss of property value due to one of the following causes:

1) physical deterioration—resulting often from wear and tear through normal use, i.e. permanently smoke-damaged kitchen or a garage that now has three or more major exits.

2) functional obsolescence—resulting from a faulty or outmoded design, such as a fenced-in master bedroom or a foyer with land mines.

3) economic deterioration—the untimely phenomenon which occurs when a house that was bought for $95,000 three years ago now has the estimated market value of a Rambler that needs body work.

door jamb
There are many homeowners in the country today who have overextended themselves by buying too much home for their income. When all their money is going toward housing, they find themselves with no money left to buy other necessities, such as food. Therefore, they are forced to resort to domainism—the consumption of one's own residence. At this point, in order to render certain parts of the home more palatable, they borrow or steal a small tin of door jamb. A rather tasty condiment, it is similar to the "house dressing" served in fine restaurants everywhere.

dormer
One who resides in multi-student housing.

down payment
A check or money order made out to the puffy coat manufacturer of your choice.

driveway
A paved storage area for your offspring's belongings.

dry closing
A closing that is successfully completed with none of the parties involved breaking into tears.

duplex
A structure containing two separate but mirror-image accommodations joined by a common wall, it is regarded as the building industry's answer to Siamese twins.

Duplex

Dutch door
1) A door divided in half horizontally, it was originally intended as a joke on America by those fun-loving Hollanders. It is of no use unless you are under three feet tall or frequently run around naked from the waist down. 2) Any door that pays for its own dinner.

E

earnest money
(a.k.a. deposit, hand money, binder) Any cash that makes a serious effort to stay in your possession and not end up in some wily broker's escrow account.

easement
The legal privilege that allows utility companies to excavate your lawn at will.

eating area
A place in a home where food may be consumed. This term generally assumes your family is accustomed to taking meals while at attention.

eminent domain
The right of the government, for the public good and with fair compensation, to run a superhighway up your gazebo.

empty nester
A person or persons whose home is without eggs.

encroachment
The unauthorized invasion or intrusion of a fixture on another's property. For instance, a foreign driveway that crosses over your property line and ends up in your garage is an encroachment. A neighboring fence that effectively seals off your den is another example. Children, while annoying, cannot be considered encroachments unless permanently installed.

Man experiencing eminent domain

Encroachment

equity

The difference between what your house is actually worth and what you owe on it. People who bought real estate before the late 1970s often have a needlepoint wall hanging that reads "Equity, Sweet Equity." Those who have purchased homes more recently using low money down loans have a different situation. Many is the homeowner of this type who has heard a loan officer say, "Why certainly, we would be happy to make you a loan based on the equity you have in your house. Now then, what kind of pen did you plan on purchasing?"

escheat

The reversion of any property (including real estate) to the state or county when the owner dies without leaving a will or heirs. However, if it can be demonstrated to the state that heirs or a will exist, the state must surrender the property. The evidence used in this procedure is commonly referred to as "escheater's proof."

escrow

The deposit of funds and/or documents with a neutral third party who promises to carry out the instructions of the parties concerned and not plan an impromptu family outing to Brazil.

expired

The state your home is in after the listing agreement runs out. This induces a multitudinous throng of agents to come forth from their dark, mysterious hiding places where they must have spent the entire time your house was on the market.

F

fallout shelter

Any form of dwelling that drops from the sky. Colloquially known as a "Dorothy Gale house," particularly if its reunion with the ground causes death to a witch.

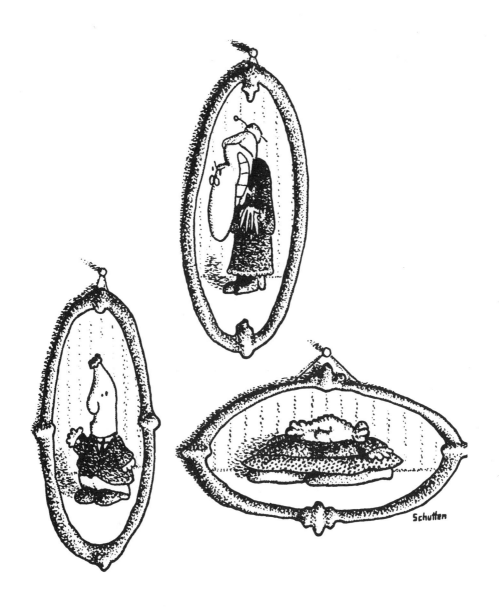

Fannie Mae and company

Fannie Mae
A vicious old crone who stoops to eking out a living by actually selling and buying other people's mortgages. She lives with her two surviving relatives, cousin Freddie Mac and idiot stepsister Ginnie Mae, both of whom are locked in the closet when company comes.

farm
1) Any large, valuable piece of land on which some pigheaded old fool won't allow a housing development citing some ridiculous dedication to feeding the world's hungry. 2) A geographic area of homes into which a real estate salesperson plants his name and face. Depending on technique and frequency, he can then reap a harvest of either sizable wealth or extreme animosity.

faucet
Device at the end of a pipe designed to magnify drip volume. Functions at peak performance during late evening hours.

FHA
The common abbreviation for the Federal Hat Agency founded in 1934 as the government's response to the nation's lack of headgear, which was causing excessive illness due to colds and resulted in a collapsed hat industry in general (although for some formal hat makers this was deliberate).

Intending to encourage the wearing of hats as a means of creating jobs, the FHA also approved a set of standards for hat construction, giving special attention to adequate brims. For a time, the FHA was extremely successful, allowing citizens to get into fedoras, skimmers and derbies they otherwise could not have afforded. In fact, with low interest rates and minimum down payments, the FHA helped millions realize the American Dream of owning one's own hat.

Recently, however, the picture has not been as bright. Due to high money costs, excessive paperwork and bureaucracy, and an inability to respond to buyer needs, the FHA is fast becoming just another ineffective government bureau. This point can be well demonstrated by traveling to any public place and observing the amount of visible hair.

The FHA helps young couples.

fireplace

Once used as a method of home heating and a place for meal preparation, the fireplace has become one of the foremost decorative and romantic status symbols in the American home. Market value can be roughly determined by noting which rooms in a home contain fireplaces. Living room and/or family room fireplaces are mandatory for marketability, and a truly upper-bracket home should have fireplaces in the master bedroom, the guest bath, and the utility room. Those unfortunates who actually have no fireplace at all have been known to compensate by purchasing a plastic log and some red and yellow light bulbs, gathering around the gas range or merely lighting some kindling in an empty living room corner.

floor plan

Planning to include a floor in your future residence is considered essential, unless you and your family can hover.

floor time

The period during which a real estate salesperson is responsible for handling telephone inquiries as well as the walk-in business for his office. Therefore, when a call is made to a real estate office to gather information on a particular property and the caller is told "Wait, Betty is on the floor, I'll connect you with her," it does not mean that Betty is easy, so don't get your hopes up.

foil

A form of wall insulation popular among those families who live in enormous potatoes.

foreclosure

A lender's way of teasing the unemployed.

formaldehyde

A chemical found in certain types of home insulation, although recently outlawed, which not only preserves the temperature within the home, but the pickled frogs in little Johnny's bedroom as well.

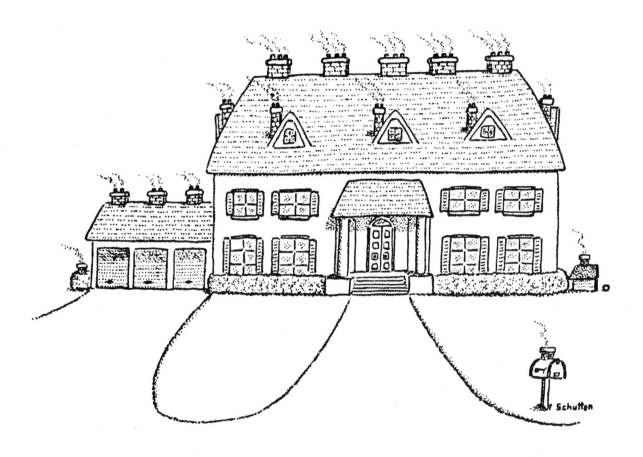

Upper-bracket home with more than one fireplace

franchise

A national fraternity/sorority for real estate brokers and agents. Unlike other fraternities/sororities, franchises try to fight that "snooty" attitude and allow anyone who can pay the initiation fee to join.

Once admitted, a "pledge" must go through a ritual of hazing, which consists primarily of being made to be seen around town wearing funny colored jackets. And although all but the most backward areas have done away with the corresponding beanies, in some regions the members must wear those same funny colored jackets for as long as they remain in the organization. Franchises are currently very much in vogue throughout the country and "fran" houses can be seen everywhere. Dues are paid to the national headquarters on a regular basis and this money is used to buy the television advertising that helps recruit new members.

front elevation

A term that has become more prominent due to an increased number of foreclosures, it involves the uprooting and removal of a home from its present location. As the mortgage holder begins to forcibly rip a home from the foundation, he always starts by putting the lifting devices under the street side of the home, then tilts the house skyward, creating the "front elevation." This is generally followed by the rear elevation and finally the carting away of the home to the lender's vault, where it is kept in storage until the deadbeat owners can cough up the overdue funds.

fuse

More expensive and less convenient version of the tinfoil chewing gum wrapper it is sometimes used in place of.

G

garage

A small building designed for automobiles to park in front of. No matter how many cars a garage is intended to hold, it won't. Nature abhors a vacuum and gets there first.

Garage, detached

garage, detached
A car house not directly connected to the main residence, a feature considered more valuable if intended. A detached garage should be architecturally similar to the home and located somewhere on the same block.

gift letter
An epistle presented to a lender by a mortgage seeker, written by a third party (usually a parent or close relative) stating that the money given to the prospective buyer to use as all or part of the down payment was not in the form of a loan, does not have to be paid back, and is in fact a gift. This term has also come to refer to any lie in print.

grandfather clause
Santa's dad.

H

handyman's special
(a.k.a. Rambling Wreck, Carpenter's Delight, The Pits, El Dumpo) This refers to any home on the market that is missing housing elements such as walls, is dirty enough to gag a maggot, or would cost more to repair than to buy.

highest and best use
The use of the land that will bring the greatest economic return. Unfortunately, this usually involves the construction of a parking lot or a porno shop.

hillside ranch
One-story house that requires lawn care via goat.

house
Not a home.

I

illiquid
Not readily converted from investment to actual cash. Real estate is considered to be an illiquid investment and is even more so in times such as these. The only way your home could be considered truly liquid would be if 1) you are willing to sell it at less than half its actual worth, or 2) your basement is flooded.

Hillside ranch

immaculate
Having nothing whatsoever to do with cleanliness, this is instead a widely employed adjective in real estate advertising meaning "on the market," or "currently for sale." Thus, sentences that read "This immaculate home . . . " or "The place is really immaculate." should actually read "This currently for sale home . . . " and "The place is really on the market."

independent contractor
Long thought to be a primal defense mechanism, many real estate agents loudly and uncontrollably bleat this phrase when asked to answer a ringing phone or attend an office meeting.

insulation
Any of a number of materials that might be used in an attempt to make a house warm without actually using heat. Insulation not only saves money by reducing the consumption of precious fuels, but some insulation can also qualify for a tax credit. The qualifying rule of thumb is this: if it adds to the beauty of your home, you're out of luck. However, if it makes your home more unattractive than it already is, you can save a bundle! You see, insulation is rated according to its repulsiveness, commonly referred to as "R" value. The more ugly an insulator, the higher the "R" value and the bigger the tax credit. This entire program was devised as a covert government action intended to counteract the effect of Lady Bird Johnson's Beautification Drive.

insulation, the installation of
There are two major points to consider before leaping into insulation, which, by the way, is not recommended. First, you must decide whether to do the job yourself or have it professionally botched. Second, you must decide what form of insulation to install.

Before running out and spending a fortune on the more conventional types of insulation, don't rule out such inexpensive alternatives as: bags of hair from barber shops; discarded clothes; and food scraps, particularly fish scales, meat fat, and poultry skin, all of which served as natural insulation for their original owners. In addition to the obvious savings advantage, these items are easy to install, have an outstanding "R" value, and will provide years of trouble-free service, aside from a certain disconcerting aroma that you will grow accustomed to, nay, even fond of with time.

ironclad contract
Any contract so carefully worded to insure absolute compliance of all parties to its terms and conditions that it can only be broken through the intercession of an extremely expensive attorney.

J

junior mortgage
A loan you are responsible for when your little boy buys a house.

K

key
This small, relatively thin strip of metal, upon being given to the real estate firm of your choice, can give access to your home and its contents to thousands of salesmen and their equally seedy customers, thus ending any semblance of privacy or security you may have previously enjoyed.

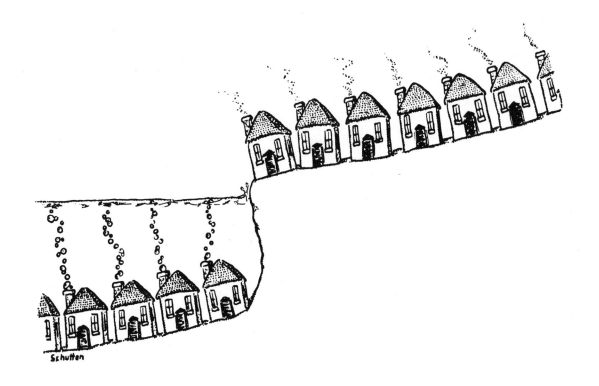

WRONG   RIGHT

Land use

kitchen

Referred to in medieval times as the hearth, this room has long held an exalted position in American homes. Primarily used for food preparation, the kitchen can also serve as an eating area, a laundry center, an office, and an important gathering place where family members can enjoy each other's company.

It is no longer considered good form, however, to view the kitchen as a kennel for one's shoeless, expectant spouse. In fact, owing to various aspects of our changing society coupled with the seemingly ceaseless demands on our time, Americans now take one out of every two meals outside the home. At present, as the popularity of the kitchen diminishes, the popularity of the large master bedroom increases. Experts feel this trend will continue until it becomes customary to perform the master bedroom's functions outside the home, which is also an ever increasing possibility.

kitchenette

Often found in small apartments or studio condos, the real estate industry's term for a hot plate and an ice bucket.

L

land

The one-third of the earth one can build houses on without drowning.

landlord

A person who owns a building for which he has not been able to arrange a condo conversion.

landscaping

Those elements in an artist's rendition of a newly constructed home that bear not even the vaguest resemblance to what is actually growing.

lawyer

An inexpensive attorney (see attorney).

Artist's
Conception

Actual
Unretouched
Photograph

Schutten

Landscaping

lease
A written disagreement between landlord and tenant, the first lease was originally devised with a deliberate and evil prejudice toward a friendly people known as Squatters. These pleasant souls had an age-old tradition of visiting property owned by another, extending a warm greeting to those owners, sitting on their haunches, and remaining in that position for many years.

leveraging
The use of small amounts of cash to acquire large amounts of debt.

library
A quiet haven of refuge in which one can enjoy reading in privacy. More commonly called a bathroom.

lien
The end result of shoddy home construction methods, it is most evident when all the furniture winds up on one side of the room and your pictures seem to hang funny.

listing
A written agreement between a property owner and a real estate broker authorizing the broker to offer the property for sale and giving him permission to appropriate thousands of dollars from the owner should a willing and able buyer happen to fall from the sky.

Listings are, in reality, the cornerstone of the industry, for without products to sell a business cannot exist. Is it any wonder then that an average homeowner will receive a minimum of 11 obnoxious pieces of mail per day and seven annoying phone calls per night, all asking the same insipid question: "Are you thinking of selling your home?"

Listings will most often take the form of one of the following:

1) open listings—the sale of homes that have no doors; 2) net listings—common in small fishing villages; or 3) exclusive right to sell listings—gives the fortunate broker, no matter who does the work, the exclusive right to get paid.

A family of squatters (see lease)

House lien (see lien)

living room
A large, carpeted display case used for lamps of questionable taste and sofas that have never been introduced to a posterior. Often, family members and other unsuitables are kept from entering this room by attack dogs and barbed velvet rope which are stationed at the entrance. In a true living room, even company will get yelled at if they spill.

lot
The form of real estate which a popular adage suggests is best obtained during youth.

M

maintenance fee
The monthly charge paid to a condominium association for the snow removal, lawn care, and repair work that has not been done.

market data approach
A method of estimating the value of a property by comparing it to similar properties that have recently sold or are currently on the market. It is the appraisal method used most often by real estate agents due to the fact that it requires almost no special knowledge or skill whatsoever, only the possession of a multiple listing book and the ability to match up the blurry pictures therein. It is often referred to as MDA. It also can be referred to as a FMV (Fair Market Value), an EMV (Estimated Market Value), a MRD (Market Data Report), a CMA (Competitive Market Analysis), a MVE (Market Value Estimate), a AVR (Assumptive Value Report), or a SWAG (Scientific Wild Ass Guess).

mechanic's lien
A ritualistic dance done by tribes of material suppliers and tradesmen after their work is completed to signify their desire for immediate reimbursement. The dance is accompanied by the following verse, sung to a familiar folk melody: "Did you ever see a mechanic lien this way and that way, did you ever see a mechanic lien this way and that?"

million dollar club
An implement of persuasion used to make people buy homes in California.

Mechanic's lien

MLS

Initials standing for Multiple Listing Service, a local organization of brokers who agree to place all listings in a common pool so that they will be uniformly wet. The MLS also puts out a sort of Sears catalog for its members to use, although customarily there is no lingerie section.

mobile home

Originally a small, flimsy, and tacky tin box inhabited by those too cheap or too poor to buy a real house. However, the mobile home industry became very sensitive to this image and in recent years has made them much bigger.

monthly gross

This is the housing industry's most perfect description of what your house payment will be—monthly and gross.

mortgage

See millstone.

N

negotiation

The art of getting the most money for a property being sold and paying the least money for a property being bought, this function is customarily performed by a real estate agent who invariably loses track of whose side he's on.

Agents are aware of the fact that negotiating is one of their most important duties and they receive extensive training to hone those skills. You can be sure that, on your behalf, your agent will be using carefully rehearsed phrases psychologically designed for maximum effectiveness such as "Take the offer, you moron, it's the only one we've seen in the 1½ years this dump has been on the market," if you are a seller. Or, if you are the buyer, "The sellers want your eldest daughter as additional down payment and I would carefully consider that option if I were you." If you are ever witness to a brace of agents negotiating, you will undoubtedly note the uncanny parallels to a dog fight: it's loud and barbaric, but if you try to interfere you'll probably get hurt. And, there is only one thing to do in either case—if it goes on too long, turn the hose on 'em.

Newel in action

neighborhood
A contiguous area containing homes of like grade inhabited by people who are not.

newel
The post that alters young children's reproductive expectations by abruptly terminating a slide down the banister.

nonconforming use
A legally permitted usage of a property that is not in accordance with current regulations, there have been many different periods of nonconforming use throughout the years. In the 1950s, we saw "beatnik buildings" that had dark shades and doorbells that sounded like bongos. The 1960s brought us "hippie homes" with long, unkempt lawns and hot and cold running drugs. At present, the most popular style of nonconforming use is "punk pads" that have huge safety pins stuck through the windows and shaved yards.

O

offer to purchase
The written proposal that a buyer makes to enter into a selling agreement with a real estate owner. Upon receiving the offer, the seller will take one of three basic options, depending largely on the price offered. He will a) accept the offer b) counter the offer c) ram the offer down the buyer's throat.

open house
The common practice of vacating your home on a given afternoon so that the neighbors can finally find out what kind of dump you live in while your real estate agent watches your television and conducts a search and destroy mission in your refrigerator.

oral contract
Any contract that is passed not from hand to hand but from mouth to mouth, they are not only invalid for real estate transactions but highly unappetizing as well.

Oral contract

P

paint
Considered the simplest way to beautify, this opaque liquid can be used to cover a multitude of surfaces within a home. Those wishing to receive top dollar for their house without incurring extravagant redecorating costs have been known to paint not only dirty walls and ceilings, but worn carpets, tacky shrubbery and unsightly family members as well.

parquet floors
An inexpensive imitation of the more popular "butter" floor, its one advantage being that it is a better conversationalist.

percolation test
The test which determines the ability of the soil to be used as coffee.

personal property
Items or things that are movable and not affixed to real estate. Personal property includes all things that a seller may legally remove from the house upon its sale, unless otherwise stated in a separate bill of sale. Some sellers have a rather warped sense of what is personal property and what is not, and have been known to take with them such easily movable items as wallpaper and duct work.

PITI
Originally an abbreviation for the components of a monthly house payment (principal, interest, taxes, and insurance), it has now come to be an expression of remorse about those same components. Example: "You pay that much for this shack? Such a piti."

planned unit development
Commonly abbreviated to PUD, a cluster-style housing similar to condominiums although easier to spell. The smaller version is known as a PUDDLE.

points
A term representing a percentage of a loan amount. As with other types of points, there are both good and bad points. Good points are the ones someone else pays. Bad points are the ones you pay.

Typical price adjustment

price adjustment
A term used by real estate agents who realize that if they asked owners to "lower the price," they would be mercilessly beaten with fireplace implements. Any price adjustment can be assumed to be in your least favorite direction.

prime rate
A figure that inexplicably has a strong effect on the real estate market, it is the current cost of a fine cut of beef.

pro rate
The hourly fee charged by a golf or tennis instructor.

procuring cause
The effort that brings about the result. If a broker can prove that a real estate sale was due to his efforts, he will be entitled to a commission. Although very few buyers would ever dream of working with more than one agent, problems have been known to occasionally arise. Agents who become involved in a procuring cause dispute are generally most gracious and considerate, settling all but a very few arguments with small but effective handguns.

prospecting
The real estate agent's method of searching for those who want to buy or sell real estate, it is the primary reason agents eat lunch with a pick and shovel, seldom shave, and have bad teeth.

Q

quaint
A versatile euphemism that can be used in place of old, small, strange, odd, run-down, or bizarre.

R

radiator
An exposed fixture made of cast iron used to heat Grandma's house, dry towels, and permanently stripe those who lean on it.

raised ranch
A style of home that forces an immediate directional decision upon entrance, making it quite unpopular with drunkards.

Real estate: earliest origins

ranch
A one-story home where suburbanites roam.

real estate
The land, its improvements, and the right to use them, real estate is most correctly viewed as a concert. Let us delve into its history, shall we?

Early man was nomadic. He tracked wild beasts, hunted fruits, stalked celery, and generally just kind of meandered around. But then one day someone discovered how to cultivate crops and domesticate animals and soon after, the following was heard: "Hey, you! You're meandering on my wheat! Quit it, or I'll have one of my cows bite off your face." Thus real estate was born.

The concept of real estate was the foundation of society and therefore, law. So, agents, next time some attorney gives you any grief, remind him of his roots and demand the proper respect. However, the concept of real estate, according to Rousseau, also "destroyed natural liberty . . . and subjected all mankind to perpetual labor, slavery and wretchedness." Then again, Rousseau didn't own any ocean front property in Monterey, either.

Realtor
A member of the National Association of Realtors, the world's largest trade association, with a membership of over 500,000, many of whom work without monetary compensation, although this is not intentional. The title "Realtor" is a registered trademark and cannot be used interchangeably with the term "real estate agent," a fact that greatly contributed to the overall length of this book.

The NAR was formed to upgrade the industry through a strict code of ethics that aspires to eliminate some of the most widely used tools of the selling profession including exaggeration, concealment, and incompetence. The other primary function of the NAR is to provide a yearly convention for its members, who otherwise would not have the opportunity to take a tax deductible vacation.

rec room
The area in which an auto body shop stores damaged vehicles.

Rollover

redlining
The practice of restricting or denying real estate loans in a specific geographic area, it is usually done by a slimy lender who skulks around a neighborhood with an enormous felt tip marker.

rent
The marvelously selfless system that allows those who don't own real estate the pleasure of paying off the mortgages of those who do.

rent control
Similar to an automatic garage door opener, this electronic device enables a landlord to raise and lower the rent by the touch of a button, and without ever leaving the comfort of his undershirt.

reproduction cost
The cost of duplicating a property that has been destroyed at current prices using similar materials. Quite different from nonreproduction cost, which is the expense of contraceptives employed to avoid the purchase of a larger home.

rock wool
A warm, hard-wearing cloth made from boulder fleece.

rollover
A stunt performed by a borrower to entice a lending institution to renew an existing loan. If the trick is not well received, the borrower may be forced to play dead.

S

savings and loan
Did you ever see the movie "It's a Wonderful Life?" It stars Jimmy Stewart as the owner of a savings and loan. Jimmy would take money from the rich people and pay them interest, then give this money to the poor (for mortgages and such) and charge them interest. Kind of like Robin Hood, no? And quite a bit more fictional. In real life S and L's aren't nearly as altruistic. Besides, Robin Hood didn't lend money to the poor, he just gave it to them. The robbing of the rich was pretty much the same, though.

At first, the spread between what the savings and loans paid the rich and charged the poor was relatively small, just enough to defray costs and provide a reasonable profit. But as time wore on, this spread became wider and wider and the savings and loans got richer and richer. All of a sudden, however, people became aware of what was happening. "They've robbed us so much, we're now the poor!" cried the rich. "If we could afford the interest they charge, we wouldn't need the money!" cried the poor. So the rich stopped giving and the poor stopped taking. And if Robin Hood had gotten as greedy, he'd have gone broke too.

second mortgage
A borrowing device used when a homeowner finds his present debt load unreasonably low and is struck with the urge to rectify the situation. Frequently encouraged to home sellers under the guise of creative financing, "taking back a second" allows them the distinct pleasure of selling their home to a buyer who has no money.

seizin
1) Actual and legal possession of real estate. 2) When preceded by the word "open," the legal right to hunt real estate. 3) A flavoring or spice used by those forced by economic hardship to eat real estate (see door jamb).

septic tank
An underground sewage container (typically made of concrete with a standard capacity of about 900 gallons) that receives waste materials from a home's plumbing system. Once inside the tank, this waste tends to separate into three parts—liquid, grease and prophylactics.

Showing in progress

shack
1) When selling your own home, the primary word used to describe every other home presently on the market. 2) To cohabit with the female residents of those homes.

shared appreciation mortgage
A home loan that forces the lender to visit you biannually and join in the positive vocal commentary on your lovely home.

shingle
Thin, rectangular pieces of wood, asbestos, asphalt, tin or slate, which are found in your yard after a storm.

showing
The art of demonstrating real estate. If you call into a real estate office looking for a specific salesperson and they tell you "Oh, he can't be reached, he's out showing," this in itself does not mean that the agent is a pervert, although the possibility is still present. It means he is performing one of his duties, which consists of driving potential buyers to a home, touring the home with them while helpfully identifying various areas and features ("Sorry to bother you, Mrs. Homeowner. This must be the bathroom, we won't be a minute. A marble tub, isn't it lovely? And so are you, Mrs. Homeowner! Can I hand you the soap?") then waiting downstairs so the prospects have the chance to talk it over and/or ransack the bedrooms.

sign
A piece of metal or board a real estate agent will implant in your front yard for the purpose of generating phone inquiries which turn into prospects who will eventually buy someone else's house. Be aware that the signs of some firms will leave a hole in your lawn large enough to contain a small child.

sill cock
1) A faucet located on the outside of the house to which a hose can be attached. 2) An obnoxious rooster that wakes you by crowing on your window ledge.

single family residence
A home that contains only unmarried people.

Man and his sill cock

slab
The flat, horizontal concrete section used as the foundation for a house. Although similar in function to a basement, it is much more difficult to panel.

sod
Rolls of grass that are, with great dignity, laid green-side-up in your yard, where they have come to die.

Southern California
Assuming utopia went condo, it would still be cheaper to buy real estate there than in Southern California. If you don't live there and would like to know what you are missing, the following will be an excellent simulation: 1) multiply your present house payment by any two-digit number and 2) go outside and pretend you can see or smell the ocean. However, in this simulation you would be missing what seems to be Southern California's major drawing card—the weather. But next time it's too cold where you live, ask yourself if you and your family would mind going without food and clothing in order to have a year-round tan.

spotless
As used in real estate advertising, refers to any home that does not have a polka dot decorating motif.

split level
A home style that was designed to satisfy the needs of an obscure sect of step worshippers who view stairs as symbolic paths to heaven ("Bhedroom") and hell ("Basemanta").

steering
A highly publicized and much maligned practice, it is nonetheless a vital function of an agent who shows property to customers via automobile.

stud
A board kept for breeding purposes.

sublease
An agreement used to rent an underwater warship.

suburb
Those communities that are found beneath the urb.

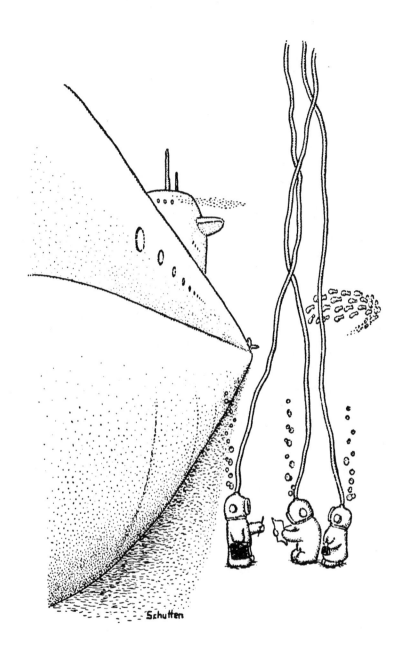

Couple signing sublease

Moob

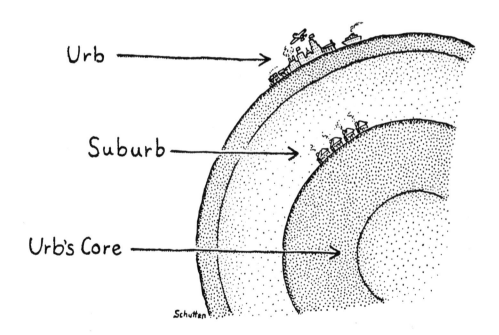

Urb

Suburb

Urb's Core

Schutten

Location of suburb

sump pump
A pump which removes water from your sump.

sweat equity
The market value of perspiration after the payment of all existing loans.

T

tenants
People who use railroad ties to hang pictures, decorate with black paint, and move during the middle of the fiscal month under cover of darkness.

termite shield
A broad piece of armor carried by a wood eating insect when doing battle with the invaders from the planet Orkin.

title
1) The ownership of real estate. 2) The evidence of this ownership, such as prematurely gray hair, an empty savings account, or an unreasonable fear of amortization schedules.

title search
As occurs during a real estate transaction, this is a frantic bout of drawer rummaging that takes place right after you are told to produce some evidence of home ownership.

tour
(a.k.a. caravan) The act of real estate agents traveling from home to home so that they may make fun of people's decorating taste while deciding where to have lunch.

townhouse
Tall, narrow residences that are built side by side so they won't tip over.

transferee
A successful, career-minded individual who, after being shown a $175,000 "handyman's special" in the approximate vicinity of his impending location, suddenly realizes why everyone else in his company already refused this particular promotion.

A boy and his sump pump

Termite in combat

turret
A small, decorative tower forming a part of a home, from which residents can fire at will toward unfriendly neighbors, or store family members with long, flowing hair.

U

utility room
The section of a dugout in which a manager keeps his extra infielders.

upgrade
1) Improvements made to a property after purchase by before closing. 2) A command used to teach a report card circus tricks.

V

vacation home
Ranging from a luxurious ocean front retreat to a tar paper shanty next to the sewage treatment plant, these are not primary residences, but second homes that provide owners a restful place to spend well deserved time off repairing the damage wrought by the people who rent the house the rest of the year.

W

wallboard
An insulation often made of vegetable fibers pressed into soft, thin slabs, it has become the product of choice due to the rising occurrence of domainism (see door jamb).

wall to wall carpeting
A carpet that totally covers the entire floor area of a room.

wall to wall carping
1) Similar to above, but done with numerous overlapping fish. 2) The act of one spouse following another to all corners of a room during a fault-finding mission.

walk-in closets
Extra spacious clothes storage area that can be entered bodily for easy access to wardrobe, etc. In some condo conversions they are renamed "studio apartments."

Turret: suggested use

Wall-to-wall carping

wall coverings

In a never-ending quest to beautify his home and surroundings, man has moved beyond mere paint and into what we in the business call "wall coverings." Some of the most common are as follows: 1) wallpaper--leading wall covering besides paint. Comes in patterns ranging from merely boring to aggressively obnoxious; 2) paneling --can create a rich, libraryish look, however only expensive wood should be used. Imitations can make even the most modest of rooms look more so; 3) mirrors--create an illusion of room enlargement. Can also add to sensuality of bedrooms. Does not work with ugly inhabitants; 4) grass cloth--gives a textured effect. Walls tend to sway in time to Don Ho records; 5) carpet--carpeting should not be used as wall covering unless you live in a van.

well

An empty hole in the ground that contained water prior to its most recent purchase.

walk to everything

Found in real estate advertising and similar to the ever popular "World at Your Doorstep," this phrase indicates that the home in question is located in the very heart of the business district wedged between the StrikeRite Bowl-A-Rama and Muley's Body Shop.

wraparound financing

1) Any form of loan that is customarily worn without a bet, or is suitable for the beach. 2) A mortgage that imitates a python by encircling the victim's wallet and putting the squeeze on it until it finally dies.

X

Legally binding document endorsement occasionally seen after over-zealous agents sell real estate to wealthy illiterates.

Y

yard

The plot of land surrounding a house designed to prevent its owner from enjoying himself on weekends.

Weather conditions on zero lot line

Z

zero lot line
A very cold land parcel boundary.

zoning
The set of local city ordinances that keeps the area you live in from looking like Houston.